ARIZONA'S SPANISH BARBS
THE STORY OF THE WILBUR-CRUCE HORSES

SILKE SCHNEIDER

Outskirts Press, Inc.
Denver, Colorado

The opinions expressed in this manuscript are solely the opinions of the author and do not represent the opinions or thoughts of the publisher. The author represents and warrants that s/he either owns or has the legal right to publish all material in this book. If you believe this to be incorrect, contact the publisher through its website at www.outskirtspress.com.

Arizona's Spanish Barbs
The story of the Wilbur-Cruce horses
All Rights Reserved
Copyright © 2007 Silke Schneider
V 6.0

Cover Image © 2007 Pascale Maslin
All Rights Reserved. Used With Permission.

This book may not be reproduced, transmitted, or stored in whole or in part by any means, including graphic, electronic, or mechanical without the express written consent of the publisher except in the case of brief quotations embodied in critical articles and reviews.

Outskirts Press
http://www.outskirtspress.com

ISBN-10: 1-59800-849-8
ISBN-13: 978-1-59800-849-4

Outskirts Press and the "OP" logo are trademarks belonging to Outskirts Press, Inc.

Printed in the United States of America

to Richard and the horses

CONTENTS

Foreword
Introduction

I. Crossing the Atlantic

    The Roundabout Journey of the Horse 1
    The First Seventeen 3
    Where did these horses come from? 8
    Where does the name "Spanish Barb" come from? 11
    What does a Spanish Barb look like? 15
    Horses multiplied in the New World 18
    Why did Spanish horses become rare? 21
    The different strains of Spanish horses today 24

II. A Rancher Strain

    A new rancher strain becomes Arizona's Spanish Barb 29
    The Wilbur-Cruce oral history 32
    Back at the newly homesteaded ranch 34
    Eva Antonia Wilbur-Cruce grows up 37
    Eva takes over the ranch 43

"Score Of Horses Reported Slain" 45
Eva sells to The Nature Conservancy 50
Rescue by the American Livestock Breeds Conservancy 52
Wilbur-Cruce horses today 61

III. Keeping Records

The Spanish Barb Breeders Association 71
The Spanish Barb in an Albuquerque museum 73

Epilogue 75
References 82
Acknowledgements 84
Websites of Interest 85
Glossary 86
Biography 88

FOREWORD

This book tells the story of the Wilbur-Cruce Spanish ranch horses.

My longtime interest and work with desert-adapted heritage breeds of livestock led me to these horses in 1997. Since then I collected information on their history from newspaper and magazine articles, books, a video-taped interview with Eva Antonia Wilbur-Cruce, museum records, rare breeds association newsletters, and personal communication with breeders, owners, admirers, critics, and descendants of the Wilbur-Cruce family and Eva Antonia Wilbur-Cruce herself; but the information was sometimes hard to find.

The goal of this book is to make this information accessible to the interested reader and to paint the picture of this colorful character, the Wilbur-Cruce horse, in the context of horse history and the conservation of endangered genetic diversity of domestic animals.

In 2005, the Wilbur-Cruce horses were formally accepted as one of the original strains by the Spanish Barb Breeders Association, a nationally respected horse breeder's organization founded in 1972.

Pilar Wilbur. (Photo © Tom Vezo)

It has been a challenge to decide on a title for the book. At the time of this writing there are about 21 different registries for horses of Spanish descent as per Colonial Spanish Horse Update "and this is likely to be incomplete" (Sponenberg 2005). The horses in the various registries come from similar genetic stock, but the registries have slightly different goals, selection criteria, historic interpretation and other reasons for forming their own registry. Since the Wilbur-Cruce strain has been formally accepted as the sixth foundation strain of the Spanish Barb Breeders Association in 2005, I have decided to call this book "Arizona's Spanish Barbs." The Wilbur-Cruce strain could also be called a Colonial Spanish Horse, registered with the Horse of the Americas and some are registered as Southwest Spanish Mustangs.

Come and explore the story of this historic character, the Wilbur-Cruce horse of Arizona, a Spanish Barb.

José Juan. (Photo © Tom Vezo)

INTRODUCTION

When I first met eye to eye with a beautiful, black Wilbur-Cruce stallion in 1997, I saw in his big, kind eyes the reflection of many memories of my own past. As my involvement with, and appreciation for, this little horse has grown over the years, I understand why this first meeting had felt like meeting an old friend.

My passion for life, for animals and their well being and for adapted breeds of livestock started a long time before ever meeting the Wilbur-Cruce horses. I will tell you a little bit about the trails my life has sometimes followed and sometimes bushwhacked until I met up with the Wilbur-Cruce horses of Arizona.

Imagine a gray, rainy, drizzly day in Hamburg, Germany. I was eighteen years old, just out of high school and it was one of the most exhilarating days in my life. I walked to the train station, leading two spirited Lipizzan horses and one little pony for the American Circus, which had just hired me on as an Elephant Rider. Just in time…the acceptance letter from University of Hanover was in the mail.

I was running away with the circus!

Together with a colorful bunch of people and animals we loaded up the train and I waved good-bye to Hamburg. Let the show begin!

My elephant number got transformed into the cowboy number and here I started working with descendants of the Spanish horses, the Lipizzans. They had changed much in type and size, but were still the agile, athletic, intelligent, surefooted mover that can adjust to the demanding circus travel and performance schedule, as long as they had "their people" to take good care of them.

Only when I met the Wilbur-Cruce horses some twenty years later and studied their history did I realize that I worked with their "cousins" in the circus; the same quick, athletic, people-loving horse with a big heart.

The circus, by the way, was named the American Circus, although the owners were Italian, and the performers were from all over Europe, Asia, and Africa. Nobody was there from America. Nevertheless, the license plates on the circus trucks were American, and the huge three-ring circus tent was decorated with stars and stripes; it was all part of the show.

The circus train and the Lipizzan horses led me to the trails in America. In the early 1980s I explored some of the American historic cowboy trails on my trusted gray Arab horse "Samir" – 1200 miles in seven weeks. We went from Santa Fe to Dodge City on the Santa Fe Trail and from Dodge City to Fort Worth on the Chisholm Trail. I was fascinated by the "Old Wild West" and the many famous and infamous characters who made it so colorful. We (the horse, the wagon master and I) had been challenged by the Caravan of Dreams Performing Arts Center in Fort Worth, Texas, to arrive at High Noon on the day of their grand opening, and if we did, after my solo ride along the Santa Fe and Chisholm trails, they would pay our expenses.

When meeting the Wilbur-Cruce horses more than a decade later, a lot of that history came alive in form of a tough little horse who still survived against all odds.

Upon completing the "Tale of Two Trails" as we called our 1200-mile adventure, I accepted an offer to work on a cattle and horse station in the vast outback of Western Australia. The station was located a few hours outside of Fitzroy Crossing, a little Aboriginal outpost. The 300,000 acre station ran cattle and horses much like the old frontier days in the southwestern United States — open range. We rounded up the 110 stock horses in the spring, as soon as the floodwaters receded. Most of the fences washed away during the floods, so it took a few weeks of daily long hours in the saddle to bring in the various bands. The feeling of absolute freedom rounding up semi-wild horses (mostly WILD) in the vast outback of Western Australia was accentuated by flocks of black and white cockatoos, pink galahs screaming with excitement, huge green clouds of budgies flying by, gigantic lizards (goannas) hissing from seemingly nowhere, crocodile eyes watching us as we rode across the river, avoiding deadly king brown snakes and many others. Magical colors at sunset and dawn…every day was worth a lifetime, every day a new adventure! The animals, plants, and nature all around me were my friends.

The Outback of Western Australia. (Photo by Richard Felger)

My job was to move the 35 or so workhorses that we had selected from camp to camp over the next three to four months. We, that is the round-up crew and the horses, lived out in the bush at the various camps. A camp consisted of a fire pit, a shelter for cooking and shade with a eucalyptus-leaf roof, and some cattle and horse pens. My job was to keep the horses healthy and happy, and in good shape, so they were ready for another buck the next day. The cowboys generally had two horses each to alternate and some back-up horses. Every morning just before sunrise, after the challenge of catching and saddling up the horses, about twelve Aboriginal stockmen, the station manager, and a couple of jillaroos (cowgirls like me) rode out. Bucking, running, twisting, snorting horses feeling good, ready to stampede any cattle in sight (needless to say, that was not the goal of the round-up, or muster, as they say in

José Juan. (Photo by Silke)

Australia), and a round of applause with lots of laughter from the Aboriginal stockmen when another young cowboy had stayed on his horse…or had fallen off…either outcome was cause for celebration just before work could begin. Remembering those days on the ranch in the Australian outback and learning the history of the Wilbur-Cruce ranch horses seemed like a total connection, an overlapping of time, a crossing of paths, memory lane: you name it. I see and ride the Wilbur-Cruce horses today and memories of the outback days connect the history of the horses with my own.

The outback station work led to another trail back in the USA. I accepted an offer to work as Animal Systems Manager for the Biosphere II project in the Catalina Mountains near Tucson, Arizona. While working on the design, construction, and daily operation of the prototype animal production system, I met the American Livestock Breeds Conservancy when I was desperately trying to find chickens that could still scratch for worms and hatch their own young. I had no idea that many of the old adapted breeds of livestock and poultry of grandpa's barnyard had virtually disappeared to make room for highly selected, intensely managed, industrial breeds. Lots of feed and labor in, lots of product out, and much infrastructure to support it all. Fortunately the American Livestock Breeds Conservancy had been working since 1977 to preserve the old breeds unique to North America. So when the Wilbur-Cruce herd was rescued in 1990 by the American Livestock Breeds Conservancy there was another crossing of trails.

In the mid 90s I graduated from the University of Arizona in Animal Science and started to work with the Tucson based non-profit organization Drylands Institute as Research Associate and Director of Desert Rare Breeds, preserving heritage breeds of livestock and poultry adapted to arid lands.

My interest in adapted livestock from the Australian outback to futuristic Biosphere II led me to the Wilbur-Cruce horses in 1997. A well adapted desert horse. Since then I have done my own field research in the United States, Germany, Austria, Africa, Italy, Hungary, Brazil, and Peru. My travels and conferences have taken me to those countries since 1997, and everywhere I found much to learn about the Spanish horse, in print, in conversation, and most amazingly in the real live horse itself.

This has been an exciting adventure. Here I tell the story of the Wilbur-Cruce horses, one strain of just one breed out of many breeds of horses. To me all horses and all breeds are heroes - unbelievably patient and kind companions, who have given their lives in war and peace, carried and pulled immense weights and carried the pioneers across unknown trails. Horses forgive our many mistakes in training and husbandry, and they give joy to so many people all over the world. This is one of many stories. Each horse has a story to tell.

Let's celebrate the horse!

José Juan and Lorenzo. (Photo © Steve Hillebrand)

I
CROSSING THE ATLANTIC

CHAPTER 1
THE ROUNDABOUT JOURNEY OF THE HORSE

60 Million years ago.
"The development of the equine species can be traced back to the small animal known as **Eohippus** [*known to modern science as* **Hyracotherium**], *which existed 60 million years ago. On the American continent the animal evolved in accordance with the changing environment, the stages of development culminating six million years ago in* **Pliohippus**, *the single-hoofed prototype for* **Equus**.*"*
(Elwyn Hartley Edwards 1994:11)

Over one million years ago horses migrated over the then existing land bridge from North America to Eurasia, where further evolution and finally domestication took place, changing history forever. Domesticated horses changed the fate of humankind. Man could travel faster, conduct wars more effectively, carry more weight, and explore new frontiers.

In 1519, with the Cortés expedition to Mexico, the first horses set foot on the American continent in Mexico. About 11,000 years earlier horses had vanished entirely from the Americas, about 1400 years after the first people arrived (Mead 2004). Horses were most probably hunted to extinction by those early humans (Martin 2005), although some controversy remains as to what really caused them to disappear. Fact is, horses disappeared from the Americas.

Some early colonies of Europeans, horses and other livestock had been established in the Caribbean following Columbus' second arrival in 1493. Horses had arrived from Spain and breeding groups were established. More horses came with later expeditions and the first recorded 17 horses (16 horses and 1 foal born aboard the ship) set foot in Mexico in 1519. It was commonplace for horses to die aboard the two to three month-long sea journeys from Spain. "Between 25 and 50 percent of the horses typically died during the trip" (Dutson 2005:12). Thus the expression "horse latitude" in the mid-Atlantic; dead horses were thrown overboard.

CHAPTER 2
THE FIRST SEVENTEEN

"Díaz del Castillo may have had, with the rest of the conquerors, a lust for gold, ...but he had more than this. He had the courage and the ability to tell the story as he knew it, and the product is a masterpiece. From the very beginning he talks about horses...he sets out to give a complete list of the horses embarking with Cortés for Mexico, with characteristic comments on their individual abilities. He says:

>...the horses were divided up among the ships and loaded, mangers were erected and a store of corn and hay was put on board. I will place all the names of the mares and horses down from memory.

Loading horses in the sixteenth century.
(From a 1769 Spanish riding manual)

Shipboard transport in the sixteenth century.
(From a 1769 Spanish riding manual)

- Captain Cortés had a dark chestnut stallion which died when we reached San Juan Ulúa.
- Pedro de Alvarado and Hernándo López de Ávila had a very good sorrel mare, turning out excellent both for tilting and for racing. When we arrived in New Spain Pedro de Alvarado took his half either by purchase or by force.
- Alonso Hernández Puertocarrero had a swift grey mare which Cortés bought for him with his gold [shoulder?] knot.

- Juan Velásquez de León also had a sturdy grey mare which we called *'La Rabona'* [bob-tailed]. She was fast and well-broken.
- Christóval de Olid had a dark brown horse that was quite satisfactory.
- Francisco de Montejo and Alonzo de Ávila had a parched sorrel, useless for war.
- Francisco de Morla had a dark brown stallion which was fast and well reined.
- Juan de Escalante had a light bay horse with three white stockings. She was not very good.
- Diego de Ordás had a barren grey mare, a pacer which seldom galloped.
- Gonzalo Domínguez, an excellent horseman, had a dark brown horse, good, and a grand runner.
- Pedro González de Trujillo had a good chestnut horse, a beautiful color, and he ran very well.
- Moron, a settler from Bayamo, had a pinto with white stockings on his forefeet and he was well reined.
- Baena, a settler from Trinidad, had a dark roan horse with white patches, but he turned out worthless.
- Lares, a fine horseman, had a very good bay horse which was an excellent runner.
- Ortíz the musician and Bartolomé Garcìa, who had gold mines, had a black horse called *"El arriero"* [he had probably driven a pack train] and he was one of the best horses taken in the fleet.
- Juan Sedeño, a settler of Havana, had a brown mare that foaled on board ship. Sedeño was the richest soldier in the fleet, having a vessel, a mare, a negro, and many provisions.

In this manner the rugged old conqueror recalled the sixteen horses that first sailed to Mexico, "…leaving a record that William H. Prescott calls 'minute enough for the pages of a sporting calendar.' Actually seventeen horses in all arrived at Vera Cruz when the foal of Sedeño's mare is counted" (Denhardt 1947:50-51).

Lorenzo. (Photo by Silke)

The above description of the 'first seventeen' is quoted from Robert Moorman Denhardt's book "The Horse of the Americas." Another translation can be found in Deb Bennet's book "Conquerors" (1998). Other translations also exist. "There has been considerable variation in translations of this section, especially with regard to color. The whole problem of color translation is extremely difficult, particularly since terms vary from section to section within Spanish-speaking countries. To further complicate the situation, there have been some changes in meanings in the same color terms since the days of the Conquistadores" (Graham 1949:56).

There is also an account of first horses to set foot onto the mainland in Panama, five years before Cortés' expedition. These horses are said to have been brought directly from Spain as well as from Española by Alonso de Ojeda and his rival Diego de Nicuesa (Bennet 1998). There appears to be no recorded details about this event and the horses apparently did not persist.

CHAPTER 3
WHERE DID THESE HORSES COME FROM?

"One thing is certain; of all the monuments which the Spaniard has left to glorify the reign in America there will be none more worthy than his horse."
(Frederic Remington, in Samuels and Samuels 1979:197)

The Spanish horse was famous all over Europe at the time of the European discovery of the New World. "The repute of the Spanish horse attributes directly to the Barb and the proximity of Spain to North Africa for continual importations… Bred for 700 hundred years in Spain for incredible endurance qualities, agility, fleetness, smooth gait and fine temperament, the Spanish horse arrived in America well suited for the tasks required of him. He was the first domestic horse bred on the North American continent" (Spanish Barb Breeders Association 1983:2). The islands of the Caribbean held the first breeding ranches of horses that were imported from Spain starting with Columbus' second voyage to the islands. From the Caribbean the horses came to the mainland (Veracruz, Mexico) with Cortés' first expedition in 1519.

There are many different historic perspectives as to where exactly the horses that set foot again on the American continent came from. Of course, from southern Spain, but what kind of horse exactly sailed across?

Some of the confusion arises from the fact that "breed" is a relatively new concept. Horses were looked at, selected, and judged by "type," not breed. Names for a certain group or strain, as we say today, were often named after a region, or sometimes a family.

The Barb horse came from the Barbary coast of North Africa to southern Spain with the Moorish invasion in 711 A.D. Some writers will argue that the horses were of Arabian type, very different from the Barb.

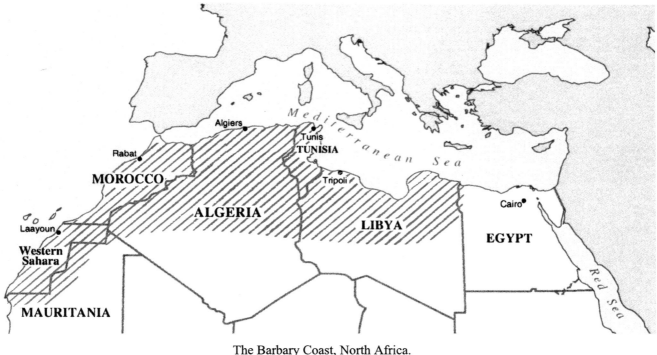

The Barbary Coast, North Africa.

"The contemporary chroniclers, historians, and poets speak only of African horses, or Moorish horses, or Barbary horses, or Tlemcen (near Oran) horses, and not of Arabian horses. …. Another indication that the best imported horses at this time were Barbs is the fact that the most famous and celebrated line of *jineta* horses that developed in Spain, those called *Guzmanes* or *Valenzuelas*, was founded by a Barb stallion, Guzmán, who was taken there by an official of the King of Morocco. ....If no other indications were present, one might even guess that the early horses were Barbs from the many contemporary illustrations that exist. In paintings and murals, the horses shown all have a tail set low in a sloping rump in the Barb fashion, while one of the outstanding features of the Arab horse is his high, level croup and his distinctive tail set" (Denhardt 1947:20-21).

I have a personnel story about this very question, a memory going back almost 30 years. In my late teens I traveled with a dear Moroccan friend to his home country, Morocco, North Africa. He always told me that he was Berber and very proud of it.

We attended the famous "Fantasia" festival, a cultural celebration of ancient Morocco. I was not really concerned about what type of horse was performing the fast moving event, for it was not the safest place for a German female teenager. Nevertheless, I told my friend Chakib "what beautiful Arabs," for that was the only horse breed I knew and worked with besides the German breeds I had ridden. My friend turned to me in disbelief and answered (in French of course) "not Arabs, Berber horses! We have Berber horses!"

CHAPTER 4
WHERE DOES THE NAME "SPANISH BARB" COME FROM?

The Barb horse came into Spain from the Barbary Coast of North Africa with the conquest of Spain by the Moors. The Barb, a hardy desert-bred horse of North Africa was faster, lighter, and more agile than the native Iberian (Spanish Peninsula) horse.

"Thus it was the Barbary horse which sailed over the straits with the Muslim invasion of Al-Andalus, and the Barb again was blended with Iberian stock to form the jennet, pride of Granada. Finally, it was this crossbred type - the jennet - which formed the foundation of the modern registered Andalusian, which until 1800 had not a drop of Arabian blood in its veins" (Bennet 1998:130).

Famous equestrian author, Baron Eisenberg, describes the Spanish horse and the Barb horse in his book "L'Art de monter à cheval ou Description du ménage moderne dans sa perfection" in the eighteenth century (Gonzaga 2004:4).

The Spanish Horse (Translation of Eisenberg 1759, in Gonzaga 2004:5):

Spanish Horse. (Baron Eisenberg, eighteenth century)

"Experience has made it well known that, without doubt, the Spanish Horse is the best horse in the world for equitation, not only because of his shape, which is very beautiful, but also because of his disposition, vigorous and docile; such that everything he is taught with intelligence and patience he understands and executes perfectly. As to beauty, it can be seen from the picture that he has a light head, lean, dry and without a pronounced lower jaw; small and well-set ears; big, expressive eyes; open nostrils for easy breathing and snorting; a supple neck held high; a fine, sparse mane; a rather wide chest and free shoulders; front legs very well made, in other words fleshy forearms, wide knees and straight cannons with clean, detached tendons; wide fetlocks, round, short pasterns, known as well-jointed, and the feet, or hooves, with good horn. His coat is the most beautiful that can be seen, and his back seems expressly made for a saddle, because his withers are high and shoulders light. He has good loins and a very well-shaped croup; a beautiful and full tail set on in a way that he always carries it with panache, giving him an impressive air: his haunches are so flexible that he sits upon them, his thighs strong and in proportion with the roundness of the croup; his hocks good and made to bend and support him, and the same in general of the rest of the hind leg. In a single word, it seems that Nature made him expressly for equitation: and in truth there is none that surpasses him in heart, magnanimity or spirit."

The Barb Horse (Translation of Eisenberg 1759, in Gonzaga 2004:12):

Barb Horse. (Baron Eisenberg, eighteenth century)

"After the Spanish Horse, comes the Barb, which is also very good for equitation, although usually smaller, not as strong, lacking the same brilliance in his bearing, and not so free in his shoulders. Even so, he does not lack quality, having good thighs and a great gracefulness at work, especially in his turns; his Terre-à-terre is one of the most beautiful amongst all horses in the world, and the suppleness of his haunches gives a lot of pleasure to his rider during execution, because he is extremely docile and has a good memory. Therefore he is easy to train, as long as it is done with kindness and discretion, and with delicate aids; but never with harshness, or long lessons, which wear out his good will, or stifle his disposition, which is in fact the best among all horses in the world."

These two types of horses then formed the Spanish Barb, the famous horses of Spain that set foot again on the North American continent after horses had been gone in the New World for over 11,000 years.

For almost 500 years, "the Spanish Barb served America as the horse of the vaquero, the frontiersman, the Indian, and the cowboy. Famed for hardiness, ability to survive, to care for himself, excellent temperament, easy ride and cow sense, his feats of strength, stamina and courage are endless. His was the blood of the original mustang of the vast American plains and also the wild horse of the South American pampas…foundation of the Criollo breed. All color phases such as the appaloosa, paint, palomino, buckskin, dun, and grullo were originally introduced to America through the Spanish Barb. His blood was used extensively in creating many American breeds. The heritage of the modern Quarter Horse traces to the Spanish Barb in the considerable use of Spanish mares in the development of the breed.

This then is the Spanish Barb. The blood of the ancients runs strong in his veins; that blood which was used throughout the world to breed-up, refine and develop many breeds. Though few in numbers, the breed remains historically important and is opening the eyes of many horsemen in its impressive comeback" (Spanish Barb Breeders Association 1983:2).

Eva Cruce. (Photos © Steve Hillebrand)

CHAPTER 5
WHAT DOES A SPANISH BARB LOOK LIKE?

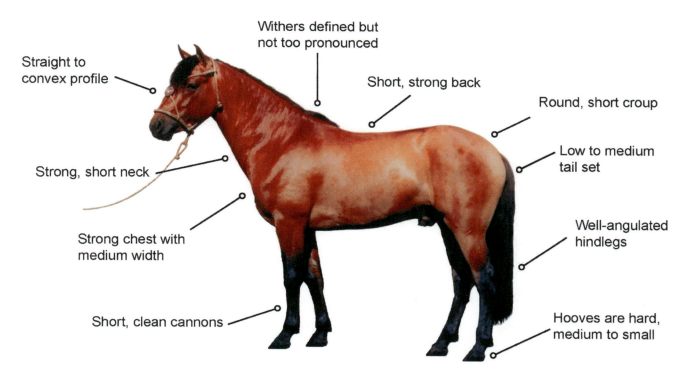

"El Torbellino," owner/breeder Jean Walsh

The overall appearance of the Spanish Barb is one of balance and smoothness with depth of neck and body, roundness of hip, short, clean legs and a well-set, distinctively refined head. Standard height of the Spanish Barb is 13.3 to 14.3 hands. A few individuals may mature slightly under or over but will not represent the norm.

All colors are found within the breed: dun/grulla, chestnut, black, bay, roan and paint (both overo and tobiano), as well as other color variants.

The head is distinctively Spanish in type; lean, refined and well formed, averaging 19 - 22 inches from the poll to an imaginary line across the top of the nostrils, with a broad flat forehead. The profile is straight or slightly convex. The ears are short to medium, curved inward and slightly back at the tips, measuring from 5 to 5 ½ inches in stallions and 1 inch longer in mares. The eyes are set well forward on the head and primarily brown, but blue eyes occur occasionally. A prominent bone structure above the eye is characteristic. The muzzle is refined, short and tapered, being set off by a shallow mouth and firm lips. The nostrils are crescent shaped and of ample size for air intake when enlarged during exertion.

The chest is strong, medium in width and sufficiently muscled inside the forearm to form an arch. The ribs are well-sprung, never slab-sided and the heart girth is deep, varying from 67 to 74 inches in circumference, depending on the height and overall size of the horse. The shoulder is well angled and in balance with the back and heart girth.

The back is short and strong, in proportion to the length of the shoulder, forelegs and depth of girth. The loin is short, straight, strong and full. The croup is round and sufficiently full in width and length to be in balance with the body. The hindquarters are not heavily muscled. The flank is deep. The tail is set medium to low.

The legs are straight, strong and well formed with long muscling in the forearms and thighs and with short, clean cannons. The bone is dense. The circumference of the front cannons average 7 ½ to 8 ½ inches. During the summer the feathering is either lacking or curled tightly against the lower leg. The joints are well developed, strong and free of excess flesh. Chestnuts on the front legs should be small, smooth and non-protruding. Chestnuts, when they appear on the hind legs, should be extremely small and flush with the leg. Ergots are either lacking, very small, or appear more as a callous. The pasterns are strong, medium in length and slope and have good flexibility which contributes to the smoothness of the gaits. The hooves are ample and well shaped, with an excellent frog formation and thick walls which are extremely hard.

Under normal conditions the mane, forelock and tail are quite long and full. An exceptionally full mane will sometimes fall naturally on both sides of the neck.

The classical style characteristic to the Spanish Barb and all Iberian/Barb-descended breeds is displayed by their natural carriage, action, intelligence and temperament under saddle. These somewhat elusive traits remain an important part of their heritage and appeal and are basic to the successful restoration of the breed (adapted from Spanish Barb Breeders Association, Breed Standard in the Studbook 1972-1982).

CHAPTER 6
HORSES MULTIPLIED IN THE NEW WORLD

In North America early explorers and settlers took the horses and other livestock northward from southern Mexico, where ranches appeared quickly after the conquest. "Close on the trail of the exploring *conquistadores* came the padres, establishing missions and gathering the native populace into *rancherias* where they could be converted… As an example, let us look at the work of Padre Kino in Primera Alta. His accomplishments as a stockman would alone have made him famous" (Denhardt 1947:104).

Many Native Americans, such as the Plains People, obtained their horses either by trade, theft or by capturing feral ones. It changed the way of many Native American people. Buffalo (bison) hunting was made easier on these sturdy, agile, fast, courageous Spanish mounts. Horse travel allowed for faster and vaster distances and larger loads, and home ranges could be protected more effectively against the new intruders. By the late 1800s feral Spanish horse herds roamed the west, numbering into the millions. "No country in the world has proved more suitable for them than the Americas. In northern Mexico and the great prairies of Texas, Arizona, and New Mexico, in fact right up to Canada, the horses brought from Spain wandered and multiplied in countless herds. But the southern Pampas seem to have been designed by nature as the ideal country for the horse" (Graham 1949:107). The spread of horses in the Americas was like a re-wilding of Ice Age animals.

Thom Cruce. (Photo © Rose Collins)

Horses went southward from Mexico and new importations from Spain contributed to the South American population. Some examples of South and Central American Spanish horses are listed below.

The Peruvian Paso horses display the smooth, lateral gait, resulting from centuries of selective breeding.

Puerto Rico's gaited horses are the Paso Finos, also selected for their smooth gaits.

The Criollo horse of Argentina is valued for its hardiness, agility, intelligence and cow sense. It is described as small but very active, ranging from 13 hands 2 inches to about 14 hands 3 inches. "Greater height is held to be a symptom of lack of purity… 'Despreciar el grande y ensillar el pequeño' ('Reject the big and saddle the small')" (Denhardt 1947:214).

"Size has been gained at the expense of stamina, an easy gait, and the capacity of bearing hardships and carrying heavy weights. After experiments of every kind had failed in the effort to produce a better cattle horse than that which nature had herself produced unaided, the government in Buenos Aires has formed a Stud Book, to keep alive the breed of the *Criollo* horse" (Graham 1949:137).

The above mentioned horses of Spanish descent are only a few examples of the vast array of Spanish stock in Central and South America.

CHAPTER 7
WHY DID SPANISH HORSES BECOME RARE?

By the mid-1800s settlers and adventurers came in from the northeast, mostly on larger mounts that were later imports from northern Europe and England. As they moved west, they encountered the native Americans on their agile, extremely fast Spanish mounts. Soon these little horses were considered "foreign" and "inferior" and many were shot, especially the stallions, to be replaced with larger breeds.

"The Colonial Spanish horse became to be generally considered as too small for cavalry use by the Anglo-Americans, and was slowly supplanted by taller and heavier types from the northeast as an integral part of Anglo expansion in North America" (Sponenberg 2005).

Many of the Native American horses were shot in order to take mobility away from the Native American tribes and to try to curb their raids on incoming settlers.

The feral herds were also considered competition by the new cattle barons, the range was to be free of feral horses and free of bison. Both the Spanish horses and bison almost became extinct in the late 1800s to early 1900s.

Remote mountain region on the old Wilbur-Cruce Ranch. (Photo by Steve Dobrott).

Some feral Spanish horse populations were able to escape into mountainous, remote regions, where they were left alone by hunters. An example of a feral strain of Spanish horse is the Cerbat herd of Arizona. Some of the Native American tribes were able to protect their horses, such as the Choctaw and Cherokee Indians, and other tribes also protected their mounts and selected for certain colors (Sponenberg 2005).

Other places where Spanish horses found refuge were some remote ranches and with individual families who kept their Spanish horses pure, for they "worked" for the region and were well-adapted by the late 1800s and early 1900s. Fortunately some individuals realized that the Spanish horse was quickly disappearing, and the first groups were gathered in the early to mid-1900s to start breeding associations to preserve this treasure.

Juanita and Silke in the Santa Catalina Mountains, Arizona. (Photo by Richard Felger)

CHAPTER 8
THE DIFFERENT STRAINS OF SPANISH HORSES TODAY

Shaped by selection, harsh environments, and geographic distances, different strains of Spanish horses developed, and are preserved by the registries. Following is a brief overview of some of the various strains in North America:

1. Feral strains - an example of a feral strain is the Cerbat Mountain horse of Arizona.
2. Native American strains - for example, the Choctaw horses of Oklahoma.
3. Mexican strains - still to be found in many remote regions of Mexico.
4. Southeastern strains - for example, the Banker pony from the outer banks of Virginia and the Carolinas.
5. Rancher strains - for example, the Wilbur-Cruce horse of Arizona.

For a complete updated account on the various strains please check Dr. Phil Sponenberg's "North American Colonial Spanish Horse Update" (2005).

Mexican horses exhibiting Spanish phenotype. (Photo by Richard Felger).

Rancher horse of the Wilbur-Cruce strain. (Photo by Silke)

II
A RANCHER STRAIN

CHAPTER 9
A NEW RANCHER STRAIN BECOMES ARIZONA'S SPANISH BARB

Some of the Spanish horse populations never went feral, such as the rancher strains, which typically were preserved for generations by a ranching family: individual ranchers who loved and appreciated the ways of these horses. Tough, small, surefooted, easy-keepers, big-hearted, courageous, intelligent, and with a strong bond to "their" people. It was an honest horse with a great disposition, just like breeders and horsemen in Europe had described it some 500 years earlier, before horses sailed off to the New World.

One of these rancher strains, namely the Wilbur-Cruce horses of Arizona, was discovered in 1989 on a remote ranch at the Arizona-Mexico border. Eva Antonia Wilbur-Cruce, a third generation cattle rancher, had fought for her little "rock horses," as she frequently called them, because of their ability to travel fast and safe over rocky terrain and because they could survive on relatively little feed and water, both of incredible importance in the desert and mountains of today's southern Arizona.

Larry and Pancho. (Photo by Silke)

A "rock horse." Juanita and Silke in the Catalina Mountains. (Photo by Pascale Maslin)

CHAPTER 10
THE WILBUR-CRUCE ORAL HISTORY

"They were brought here from Rancho Dolores in Mexico, the headquarters of Father Kino, who had brought them from Spain - a fine breed of Barbs that were brought to Spain by the Moors" (Eva Antonia Wilbur-Cruce 1987:107).

Oral history from the Wilbur family tells the story of Juan Zepulveda, a horse trader from Sonora, Mexico, who brought 600 head of horses to the Territory (today Arizona) in the late 1800s on his way to the stockyards in Kansas City. The origin of these horses was the Rìo San Miguel area, 110 miles south of Nogales, Sonora, where Father Kino had built his headquarter mission, Nuestra Señora de los Dolores (Mission Dolores), starting in 1687.

Rounding up horses on the Wilbur Ranch around 1900. (Courtesy of Arizona Historical Society).

At Mission Dolores Father Kino produced the finest breeding stock of cattle, sheep, goats, and horses. His talent and ability as a superb livestock breeder are legendary. From his headquarters Father Kino supplied the other missions that were being established. He also supplied Native Americans and trained them in animal husbandry and breeding techniques, as they converted to Christianity and "promised to live a peaceful life." Other tribes, such as the hard-riding, always-on-the-move Apaches, regarded the missions' ranches as fabulous "supermarkets" and often helped themselves to livestock, especially horses.

This is where Juan Zepulveda's horses are said to have originated, descendants of Father Kino's fine Spanish Barbs.

CHAPTER 11
BACK AT THE NEWLY HOMESTEADED RANCH

Dr. Reuben A. Wilbur, a graduate of Harvard Medical College, came to the Territory to work as a physician for a mining company near the town of Arivaca, near the border between Arizona and Mexico. The mine was soon shut down due to too many Apache raids and Dr. Wilbur decided to homestead one of the first ranches in the area around 1868.

The old ranch house. (Courtesy of Eva Antonia Wilbur-Cruce)

Horse trader Juan Zepulveda would pass along around 1870 with his horses for sale from the Mission Dolores area in Mexico. Dr. Wilbur bought his first herd of twenty-five mares and one stallion from Juan Zepulveda, and that founded the Wilbur ranch horse herd (you see later why the name changed to Wilbur-Cruce). The horses lived, worked, and multiplied on the ranch, left much on their own to survive. Only the ones needed for work were corralled and trained as was common in those days.

The old mesquite corral. (Courtesy of Eva Antonia Wilbur-Cruce)

"The Spanish horses thrived in the desert and were the horses of the day. They were our companions from sunup to sundown and sometimes deep into the night, year in year out. They had speed, stamina, and intelligence, and, strange as it may seem, they had feelings" (Wilbur-Cruce 1987:107).

Juanita. (Photo © Steve Hillebrand)

CHAPTER 12
EVA ANTONIA WILBUR-CRUCE GROWS UP

Eva Antonia Wilbur-Cruce was Dr. Wilbur's granddaughter. Her father married a woman from a prominent Mexican family and Eva was their first born child in 1904.

Reuben Wilbur, Eva's father, was reclusive and isolated the family on the ranch. In some sense this might have saved the horses, for it was already common practice in the early 1900s to crossbreed the Spanish horses with larger breeds, by shooting and replacing Spanish stallions. The Wilbur herd stayed pure, living an isolated life with a reclusive ranching family.

The ranch was and still is beautiful. The small Wilbur ranch house stands alone next to a forest of enormous cottonwood trees along a creek. An old mesquite corral bordered the house. In 2006 the corral could still be seen, as well as the ruins of the old ranch house. It's a beautiful peaceful place, to sit under the old cottonwood trees that witnessed the original herd come to water and gallop through the dry creek bed. From there deep trails take off over the mountains, made by thousands of horse hoofs over 130 years of

Eva on horseback with rifle at age 13.

(Courtesy of Arizona Historical Society)

the Wilbur-Cruce ranch operation. Feed was sparse through much of the year, and the sparse forage helped select the herd's strongest most efficient horses over the years. Predators like mountain lions also kept the numbers down and selected for the fastest, most intelligent horses to escape lion claws.

The old Wilbur ranch house among cottonwood trees.
(Courtesy of Arizona Historical Society)

The old Wilbur ranch house. (Photo by Steve Dobrott)

Eva Antonia Wilbur-Cruce recalls her early years on the ranch in a book she wrote in her 80s, "A Beautiful Cruel Country." She describes the hard ranch life in isolation. The Wilbur children were schooled at home and worked hard on everyday ranch chores. Eva developed an incredible bond with her best friends, the animals. The best of all were the horses, especially her first horse named Diamante. She talks a lot about Diamante in her book. She praises her little rock horses, as she often calls them.

"Damian and I both knew all about the intelligence and ability of the little Spanish horses. We sometimes called them rock horses because they were surefooted on rocky surfaces, and the Indians called them doghorses because of the doglike devotion they had for their masters" (Wilbur-Cruce 1987:223-224).

She recalls her first ride up the mountain as a very young child, behind her father on his (later her own) horse Diamante.

Ruby Wilbur, early 1900s.
(Courtesy of Eva Antonia Wilbur-Cruce)

She was terrified going over extremely steep, rocky trails up and up the mountain. Her father explains that the horse is surefooted and won't fall down. After reaching the top of the mountain "El Cerro," Eva recalls an extreme sense of happiness and accomplishment. A moment, she will "never forget." This moment gives her a new look at the horse that carried her to this happy memory, not to forget that Eva is only 5 years old.

"I was now seeing Diamante in a different light. He was no longer just a horse. He was a friend, our companion and helper" (Wilbur-Cruce 1987:59).

Eva also recalls stories about grandfather Wilbur, who at one time "brought fine Morgan horses from Colorado, but they didn't survive" (Wilbur-Cruce 1987:107). In another scene on the ranch, Eva describes how her horse Diamante saved her father from a charging cow during a cattle branding. (All the Wilbur livestock carried the E/W brand, registered in the firstborn daughter's initials in 1904.) The cow started charging Eva's father while Eva was sitting on Diamante's back watching the branding. Diamante picked up the danger and the scene developed as follows: "I felt Diamante jump, almost spilling me to the ground. In a split second Diamante had thrown himself between Father and the cow, striking the charging animal's shoulder and shoving her forward. The cow stumbled to her feet again and took off, dragging two ropes, while two horsemen went after her. …. 'What a brave little girl! How did you think so fast, muchachita?' [asked the cowboys in amazement]...But poor Diamante. My horse stood with his head down, still laboring for breath. No one praised my little rock horse. Only I knew that he was the real hero, and that I stole his credit" (Wilbur-Cruce, 1987:223).

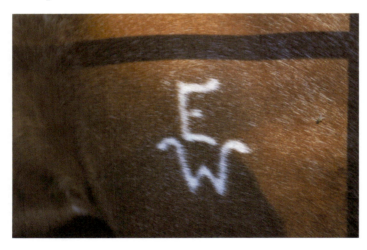

The brand. (Photo © Steve Hillebrand)

In 1918, at the age of 14, Eva was sent to attend a convent school in Los Angeles. It was a huge culture shock for young Eva to leave behind her only friends, the animals, especially Diamante, to go off to new adventures. The first year was spent shedding lots of tears but an adaptable, intelligent, curious young girl soon discovered the joys of conversation (with people for a change), and she discovered the joys of writing. Back at the ranch Eva had longed to write poetry and had done so at times in secret, for it was not encouraged by her father. Ranch work had to be done, fences mended, water holes cleaned, cattle doctored, horses broke, and poetry had no place in the world which her father so strictly protected. Now, in Los Angeles, Eva could write as much as her heart desired, she even had strong support and encouragement from one of her teachers.

For a short time Eva went back to the ranch, before attending college in Los Angeles, but sadly Eva remembers that "the animals didn't know me anymore, so I was quite bored." (Banks 2002:15).

Branding horses in the mesquite corral. (Courtesy of Eva Antonia Wilbur-Cruce)

This could have been the end of Eva's ranch life, and possibly of the old Wilbur horse herd, but fate turned a different direction in 1933.

Roping a bighorn sheep. (Courtesy of Arizona Historical Society)

CHAPTER 13
EVA TAKES OVER THE RANCH

In April of 1933 Eva was notified that her father had died following injuries when he was thrown from his horse at the Wilbur ranch. Eva rushed home and being the only child interested in the ranch, she took over ranch management following her father's death. Little did she know that she was thrown right in the middle of a raging cattle war between her late father and a neighboring cattle baron.

She was soon convinced that neighboring ranchers were trying to drive her away because of the precious Wilbur ranch water resources. - Very possible, because water is gold in the desert.

In November of 1933, Eva met her husband Marshall Cruce on a shopping trip to Tucson. From then on the ranch and the ranch horses were known by the name "Wilbur-Cruce."

For the next ten years on the ranch the war raged! Fences were found cut, horses shot, cattle stolen. Eva's nickname was "La Pistolera," acquired because of her loose gun. According to some accounts the horse herd dwindled from over 700 head to as few as 70 head during some of those years. One story even made it as far as a Los Angeles newspaper. "Score of Horses Reported Slain - Wholesale Slaughtering In Arivaca District Is Rumored Here" (Los Angeles Examiner 1933). Unidentified ranchers had driven part of the horse herd into a canyon on the ranch and machine gunned them down. Many, many dead horses were found all over the ranch by Eva and Marshall, shot right between the eyes.

Lorenzo. (Photo © Steve Hillebrand)

CHAPTER 14
"SCORE OF HORSES REPORTED SLAIN"

(October 19, 1933, Los Angeles Examiner)

The article reads:

Tucson, Arizona:

Wholesale Slaughtering In Arivaca District Is Rumored Here

Sheriff John F. Belton today pushed the investigation of a reported wholesale slaughtering of horses in the Arivaca district as rumors continued to drift in from the grazing territory that at least 50 animals, the property of the Augustine Wilbur ranch, had been driven into a canyon and shot.

The deceased rancher's daughter first reported the mysterious disappearance of the horses, remarking that she believed they had been stolen, and a few days later the sheriff received reliable information that the animals had been driven away and literally butchered.

Early this week, Undersheriff C. B. Farrar and Deputy Gus Vasquez went to Arivaca to investigate the reports. They were directed to a canyon where the slaughtering allegedly occurred, but the trip met with failure. Yesterday, however, another report was received to the effect that the horses were trapped 15 miles from Arivaca and shot.

Officers, headed by Sheriff Belton, will make a second trip to the ranch country this week.

Sheriff Belton was reluctant to discuss the rumors, stating that he would rather await the results of the investigation, but he admitted he placed credence in the reports because of the reliability of the persons who have called the matter to his attention.

In 1997, when I asked Eva Antonia Wilbur-Cruce about this newspaper article and her memories of that time, Eva's answer was: "What made me really mad is that the newspaper did not mention that I shot two of their cows for each horse they shot," followed by a cheerful giggle. It appeared that Eva had a good idea who did the dirty deed. Eva also said that she had written a second book about those cattle wars and exposed the people involved, but did not want it to be published until after her death. "It will make some people very mad," she said. Eva passed away in 1998, yet the book was never found.

The horses had barely survived droughts, shootings, and near starvation, when another event almost put an end to the Wilbur-Cruce herd.

The story goes as follows: Eva owed mortgage payments on her ranch, which she couldn't pay. The only way she could make some quick money to save the ranch was to sell her beloved rock horses. According to the story and Eva's memories, she and a few cowboys drove the herd to the little town of Arivaca. Eva had made an agreement with a neighboring rancher to sell the horses for a certain price and to meet him in Arivaca. He was to bring the money and she would bring the horses. When Eva got to town, the man broke the deal by offering only a small fraction of the pre-arranged price. Eva was furious and had her cowboys turn the horses loose. They ran back to the ranch, over 30 miles away.

Angry about the broken deal, happy to have saved her horses and most certainly worried about the future of the ranch, Eva cautiously and suspiciously later accepted an offer for help from one of the same cattle baron's cowboys. Who could trust such offer after having been lied to and let down by this man's boss? Having not much of a choice, Eva accepted the cowboy's offer, which simply stated that he'd give her the money to pay off the ranch mortgage. No strings attached, no horses to be sold, just like that. The next day this cowboy came up to the Wilbur-Cruce ranch at sundown. He simply gave her the money wrapped in some cigarette paper. He stood by his word. Apparently this compassionate cowboy felt that Eva had been set up all along and he wanted to help, so he did. His action saved the ranch and the horses.

In the year 2001, I happened to stop at a little museum in the town of Florence, between Tucson and Phoenix. By this time our own Wilbur-Cruce herd had grown to three mares and two foals. Florence is a quaint little town attached to several large prisons. The museum exhibits, among many other items, pictures of famous inmates and what their last wishes were for a meal. The museum's curator noticed that I seemed to be looking at nothing else but old saddles, old horse pictures, spurs, saddle blankets and other horse-related items. The lady asked what brought me to Florence and if I would like to see the prison section of the museum. I was happily looking at old horse photographs, comparing their sometimes pronounced Spanish types to our present Wilbur-Cruce horses and I proudly explained to her that we own and breed a very historic line of Spanish horses, the Wilbur-Cruce horses. The nice lady almost fainted, "the Wilbur-Cruce horses? We were just talking about the old lady today. She,

La Reina de la Cruce. (Photo by Silke)

Eva Antonia Wilbur-Cruce, was in our prison in 1943. She and her longtime cowboy, Luiz Lopez, were accused of killing a mare belonging to another rancher and branding her colt as her own. Mrs. Wilbur-Cruce always maintained that it was her own mare who had broken her neck when she jumped a corral fence."

Luiz Lopez. (Courtesy of Eva Antonia Wilbur-Cruce)

Tucson Daily Citizen reports in the Friday evening edition on December 18, 1942:

> *"Mrs. Cruce And Cowboy Facing Superior Court*
> *Pair Bound Over For Trial Of Charge Of Branding Another's Colt*
> *Mrs. Eva Antonia Wilbur-Cruce, operator of an Arivaca ranch, and her cowboy, Luiz Lopez, were subject of a preliminary hearing in justice court today to determine whether they would be bound over to the superior court for trial. Both stand accused of branding a six months-old colt and shooting the mother of the animal to conceal ownership of the pair. ...."*

Around Eva's prison sentence are just about as many stories as there were horses on the ranch. Some say that she deserved her prison time, others say that she was set up, again, by her rivals, the neighboring cattle baron, who bought up most of the smaller homesteads for his cattle empire. Eva was released from prison nine months later and according to those close to her, a changed woman. "Family members acknowledge that prison made her a harsher woman, and it made the .32 on her hip a permanent fixture" (Banks 2002:14).

CHAPTER 15
EVA SELLS TO THE NATURE CONSERVANCY

In 1989, Eva sold the 1,641-acre ranch to The Nature Conservancy, after her husband Marshall passed away. The ranch then became part of the 112,000-acre Buenos Aires National Wildlife Refuge, managed by the U.S. Fish and Wildlife Department. Eva's understanding was that the horses would remain on the ranch, but in 1990 the horses were to be removed due to a harsh drought and conflict with the preserve's goals.

Stewart Udall, former Secretary of the Interior, was quoted in a newspaper article (The Arizona Republic) that he saw nothing incompatible in keeping the Spanish mustangs on a portion of the Buenos Aires National Wildlife Refuge (Allen 1990).

Fortunately Steve Dobrott, a biologist on the neighboring preserve and his wife Janie, had read Eva's book "A Beautiful Cruel Country" (published in 1987 by the University of Arizona Press) and they made the connection to the famous line of Spanish horses brought up to the Territory by Juan Zepulveda from the region of Father Kino's Mission Dolores. Steve contacted Spanish horse registries, which in turn alerted the American Livestock Breeds Conservancy, and a conservation program was born for the ranch and for the Wilbur-Cruce Spanish ranch horses.

Horses on the Wilbur-Cruce Ranch before the round-up. (Photos by Steve Dobrott)

CHAPTER 16
RESCUE BY THE AMERICAN LIVESTOCK BREEDS CONSERVANCY

The American Livestock Breeds Conservancy is a well established and highly regarded conservation organization, dedicated to the preservation of rare breeds of livestock and poultry unique to North America. This organization has been working since 1977, when the concept and need for biodiversity in farm animals was virtually unknown and the rapid loss of farm animal diversity progressed almost unnoticed.

Dr. Phillip Sponenberg, DVM, Ph.D., Technical Coordinator for the American Livestock Breeds Conservancy since 1978, Spanish horse expert and enthusiast, and veterinary pathologist and geneticist at Virginia Polytechnic Institute and State University in Blacksburg, flew out to Tucson in the fall of 1989 to visually inspect the horses on the ranch (as close as he could get to the flighty herd). He met with experts from Spanish horse registries and they traveled out to the ranch, some two hours drive from Tucson.

According to Dr. Sponenberg there are three main steps to find and to secure pure strains of Spanish horses:

1. Visual inspection, phenotype. Do they look like a Spanish horse?
2. History. What is the horses' history? Do they have a history of relative isolation? Is there an oral history where the horses came from?

3. Blood typing. Does the blood typing show certain Spanish markers? Does it prove relative isolation of the herd? Does it show genetic diversity?

"Bloodtype and DNA techniques have some limitations in that no breed or herd is uniform for the presence of what are generally considered to be 'Iberian' markers (or bloodtypes). These techniques do offer great help in verifying the initial results of historic and phenotypic analysis, but are by themselves insufficient to arrive at a final conclusion. Almost invariably when the history and phenotype point to a consistently Iberian population, the blood typing and DNA evidence likewise point in this direction" (Sponenberg 2005).

Pilar Wilbur and La Reina de la Cruce.
(Photo © Rose Collins)

The team of horse experts and enthusiasts together with the Buenos Aires National Wildlife Refuge biologists took off in search of the horses. They climbed over rocks, up steep treacherous mountain paths, through mesquite thickets and cactus, and it was hot. Only a person who is used to hiking southern Arizona's mountains and deserts can understand the immense drive and motivation that all of these people must have had in common. A tough search. Many of the bands took off at the sight of people, yet the first inspection team felt excited and satisfied with their initial findings. Satisfied enough to continue their program. "The horses looked as if they'd walked right out of the past - 14 to 15 hands high, and in every shade of black, chestnut, bay, gray, and paint. Their looks matched their history precisely and I knew that these were unique animals that American Minor Breeds Conservancy (this name was later changed to The American Livestock Breeds Conservancy) should work to conserve" (Sponenberg 1990).

The team came back a second time in early 1990 and got an even closer look at the various horse bands, because a drought made the horses gather at the only water source along the creek. During this initial inventory young foals would sometimes disappear, probably fallen prey to hungry mountain lions. A few were also stolen by "treasure hunters," who had heard about the horses in the media that now exposed the story.

Horses on the Wilbur-Cruce ranch before the roundup.
(Photo by Steve Dobrott)

The Spanish horse people and the American Livestock Breeds Conservancy wanted them left on the ranch where they had roamed and adapted so well over 130 years. Their hope was to leave all of them, or at least a large portion under managed conditions on the ranch.

"We are certainly most interested in having them (remain) on the refuge. We want them to stay there as a managed herd, not a wild herd" (Sponenberg 1990). Tucson Citizen (Allen 1990), "Mustang herd nears its last roundup" The Fish and Wildlife management wanted the horses off the ranch, because they feared competition with ongoing wildlife conservation and research on the ranch.

"…U.S. Fish and Wildlife Service wants the approximately 100 horses removed from the Wilbur-

Cruce Ranch, recently acquired for the service by The Nature Conservancy. A couple of organizations dedicated to the preservation of horses with Spanish lineage disagree" (Turner 1990).

Horses on the Wilbur-Cruce ranch before the roundup. (Photo by Steve Dobrott)

The horses were to be removed and quickly. The drought had taken its toll on the remaining herd, very few foals and yearlings remained, water was sparse, predation high, feed almost non-existing. Some of the horse enthusiasts wanted the preserve to open its gates to the neighboring lush grasses on the Buenos Aires National Wildlife Refuge, at least temporarily, but the Refuge wanted them off the land because they had no specific instructions to keep and manage horses. "But if the horses were removed and sold at auction, the unique bloodline would be lost through dispersal or slaughter" (Sponenberg 1990). Eva donated the entire herd to the American Livestock Breeds Conservancy, thanks to Phil Sponenberg.

The American Livestock Breeds Conservancy stepped in to raise the funds for the safe removal of the horses and under Dr. Sponenberg's leadership the program began.

"Direct conservation is what AMBC [American Minor Breeds Association] is all about, but rescue projects can be expensive. The Wilbur-Cruce horse project, for example, cost $14,000. Special donations received so far have totaled $9,000. We need your contributions to support direct conservation programs" (Sponenberg 1990).

In the soaring heat of July 1990, the horses were trapped at the only remaining water

Horses on the Wilbur-Cruce ranch before the roundup.
(Photos by Steve Dobrott)

source in the old mesquite coral, band by band. A group of cowboys would then rope and separate any stallions and take them out to keep the mares and foals (if they were lucky) on their own. The horses were then moved to a temporary holding facility. This went on until all 77 horses were caught and safely put into pens. According to the records, only one mare was lost during this adventure, and this emaciated mare had an advanced case of skin cancer. The horses were then moved to a facility at Old Tucson, a movie back-drop and tourist attraction near Tucson, with wonderful holding facilities. The blood typing work was done at University of Kentucky under the leadership of Dr. Gus Cothran world renowned scientist (now at Texas A&M University). Dr. Cothran's equine genetics work includes feral, wild, and unusual populations of horses around the world. Fortunately the blood work came back to show that phenotypic inspection as well as Wilbur history was most likely accurate and this was indeed a herd of fairly isolated, well adapted, pure descendants of Spanish stock with good genetic variability.

At the watering hole. (Photo by Steve Dobrott).

"The blood types proved that the Wilbur-Cruce horses are indeed a unique population with a long history of genetic isolation. The few outside horses that had been introduced (such as two tattooed racing Quarter Horses found at the round up, presumably victims of rustlers) had made no discernable genetic impact" (Sponenberg 1990).

Trapping and sorting the horses in 1990. (Photo by Steve Dobrott)

Since this project had to be pulled off in a hurry due to the drought and politics involved, Dr. Sponenberg did not have much time to identify many horse breeders. He chose breeders that he knew would continue the line of Wilbur-Cruce Spanish ranch horses. The various breeding groups were chosen by phenotype and blood typing to assure the maximum genetic diversity.

Trapping and sorting the horses in 1990. (Photo by Steve Dobrott)

One group went to central Arizona, one to New Mexico, two to Oklahoma, and one to California. Extra stallions that were not of breeding quality were gelded and sold at public auction at Old Tucson. Eva Antonia Wilbur-Cruce, then 86 years of age, in a wheelchair after a recent stroke, attended this day to see her beloved horses go to new caring owners who had pledged to continue the line of her rock horses. Eva also asked that the horses should not go to cold climates, since they were so well adapted to the desert.

What a day that must have been for her! So many memories of the old ranch life and her beloved friends, the horses. A new beginning in a changing world.

Tubac and Pancho at the Dragoon Mountain Ranch, Arizona, 2002. (Photo by Silke)

CHAPTER 17
WILBUR-CRUCE HORSES TODAY

After the horses were removed from the ranch and various breeding groups were started, two Spanish horse registries took the Wilbur-Cruce rancher strain into their registries.

One was the Southwest Spanish Mustang Association in Oklahoma, the second was the Spanish Barb Breeders Association in Florida. Since then a third registry has accepted the Wilbur-Cruce strain, namely "The Horse of the Americas," which serves as an umbrella organization for the various Spanish horse registries.

Lorenzo and José Juan playing. (Photos © Steve Hillebrand)

At the Spanish Barb Breeders Association meeting in 2005, the Wilbur-Cruce strain was formally accepted as the sixth foundation strain of the Spanish Barb horses. This decision was based upon a renewed inspection by two of the Spanish Barb Breeders Association inspectors in 2003 to assure quality offspring from the foundation horses.

In 2006 we find populations in Arizona, New Mexico, Colorado, Oklahoma, California, and Nebraska. Several of the owners and breeders continue to breed their horses in natural herds on large ranches, which assures keeping the great traits of the horses alive. Breeders work together to keep the diversity of the herd intact. By then we had a good foundation herd of the Wilbur-Cruce strain (about 140 animals with the various registries), and some breeders were starting to breed their horses to the other original strains of the Spanish Barb Breeders Association. Some people who are interested in starting a small breeding group have asked if one has to have a big ranch to get involved in the breeding program. The answer is "No". We have very successful horse breeders who are raising a couple of foals every year on 5-acres or less.

At our Desert Heritage Breeds farm near Tucson, our foals are ponied out in the mountains to get lots of exercise. They know mountain bikers, crowds of

Heidi Collings and her horses at Dripping Springs Ranch, New Mexico. (Photo by Silke)

people, horse trailers, and many visitors to the corrals. The horses do well on large ranches or small holdings as long as they are not alone. They are very social and prefer living in a herd, even if the herd is only two horses plus the humans.

The Stronghold Herd at the Dragoon Mountain Ranch, 2002. (Photo by Silke)

The horses are being used in endurance and competitive trail riding, dressage, jumping, cattle and buffalo round-ups, mounted shooting events, historic parades, fairs, live exhibits and presentations, and not to forget, as wonderful surefooted, people-loving trail horses.

The challenge will be to not change the breed, but to recognize and value and preserve their strengths and local adaptation. Selecting for increased size is one of the major temptations. People nowadays are often bigger and bigger horses are often a more marketable item. Some argue for example that the Wilbur-Cruce population was probably stunted due to very scarce food much of the times. That may be true, as it is for all livestock that has scarce food resources. Some Indian ponies were reported to have reached only 12 to 13 hands, due to hard work at a very early age and few groceries. "Some of the Indian mounts were only twelve and thirteen hands and could truly be classified as 'ponies.' Obviously, harsh conditions, poor grazing, and overwork at an early age all played a part in limiting the size of the animals" (Ryden 1999:85).

With appropriate feed, the Spanish horse will get bigger than the ones left to their own devices in the deserts or mountains, yet the size is still limited by the breed itself, which is small. 13.3 hands to 14.3 hands is the accepted average by the Spanish Barb Breeders Association, with some individuals taller or shorter,

Juanita and Pilar Wilbur at the author's ranchito in the Catalina Mountains. (Photo by Silke)

Lorenzo with his new owner and friend
Beth Mann in Catalina, Arizona, 2005.
(Photo by Silke)

Pilar Wilbur and Richard.
(Photo by Silke)

but not representing the norm.

"The average figure for what are now considered to be 'small' horses - those standing under 15 hands and weighing under 1,000 pounds - nearly equals the 'wild' figure. This is not surprising in light of the fact that there were *no horses on Earth larger than this until 500 years ago*. What we consider 'small' horses actually defines the norm for the species" (Bennett 1988:78-79).

Look at the Shetland pony: you can starve it and it will be extremely small, you can overfeed it and it will be bigger, in both cases unhealthy and unhappy, but it will always be within the limits of the Shetland pony, it will not be 15 hands, or it is not a Shetland pony.

Pilar and Silke on a competitive trail ride.
(Photo by Richard Felger)

It is often amazing why people want to change breeds at all cost. If a person wants a big, tall horse, why not get a breed of horse that is big and tall? It seems so much simpler. There are wonderful breeds of horses, all sizes, colors, and talents.

The similarities of how the Spanish horses were described in Europe some 400 years ago, then described by ranchers such as Eva Antonia Wilbur-Cruce almost 100 years ago and are now described by the breeders, owners, and enthusiasts of today are remarkable. There is hope that our children and grandchildren will ride and treasure the same little horses for many generations to come.

Rick Levin on Esteban at the Dragoon Mountain Ranch competing in mounted shooting.
(Photo by Marjorie Dixon)

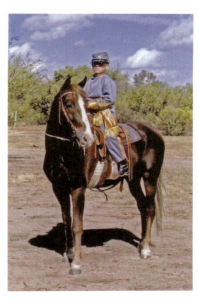

Brigette Dumais on Galan and Derek Dumais on Azul; historic parades, De Anza Days at Tubac, Arizona, 2005. (Photo by Marjorie Dixon)

Janie Dobrott on Pitiquito at the "corrida," Dragoon Mountain Ranch, 2004. (Photo by Silke)

Sierra Bonita Cruce (SiSi) and José Juan.

(Photo © Tom Vezo)

Madelaine and Josefina. (Photo by Silke)

Madelaine and La Reina. (Photo by Silke)

La Reina and Silke. (Photo by Richard Felger)

Author's mother and Josefina. (Photo by Silke)

III
KEEPING RECORDS

CHAPTER 18
THE SPANISH BARB BREEDERS ASSOCIATION

The Spanish Barb Breeders Association is not merely a registry concerned with certifying and numbering Spanish Barb horses. Its concern to accurately preserve the Spanish Barb has led to registration procedure different from other horse registries. Undesirable horses are not eligible for registration and breeders therefore must practice careful selective breeding.

"The Spanish Barb Breeders Association (SBBA) began with approximately 30 animals from which to perpetuate the breed. The merits and faults of each animal were noted and thus direction was given to the breed programs. From 1972 to 1982, the results of this planned breeding procedure are evident. The horses continue to improve in Breed Standard quality due to breeder/membership who are totally committed to the preservation of these historic animals by building through proven bloodlines, sound breeding programs, and strict adherence to the Breed Standard. Retaining the quality and the unique characteristics of this breed is the prime prerequisite.

The Association is also strict in its expectance of its breeder's integrity in recognizing and culling any individual that is not a quality representative of the breed. The SBBA feels very strongly that it is far better to cull horses in the present than to be faced with the serious problem of inferior or nonrepresentative stock in future generations" (Spanish Barb Breeders' Association 1983:1).

The SBBA remained an "open" registry, meaning that new strains of horses of Spanish descent or individuals with strong Spanish characteristics are allowed in the registry after the inspection process. This is how the Wilbur-Cruce strain, for example, was admitted. Continued inspections of offspring then allowed the Wilbur-Cruce strain to be admitted as one of the foundation strains.

Every registry has their own process of admitting horses, some are "closed" registries, i.e., no new stock after a certain year, others are "open."

Foundation stallion Padre teaching respect to youngster Pancho. (Photo by Silke)

CHAPTER 19
THE SPANISH BARB IN AN ALBUQUERQUE MUSEUM

"Standing in the Albuquerque Museum of History, Art and Science is an exact replica of the horse that carried the Spanish Conquistadores on their unequalled explorations. Displaying the perfect fit of the sole existing, full set of horse armor ever found intact in this country, and bearing a fully-armored Spanish soldier on its back, this model is the focal point of a permanent display.

The museum's curator was looking for a model to make a horse sculpture for the exhibit. The Spanish Barb Breeders Association (SBBA) was contacted, being the only Spanish Barb registry in the country at the time.

The measurements of the horse were taken directly from the average measurements in the SBBA files in 1982. This exhibit was completed in 1983.

The armor was placed on the horse sculpture and it fit perfectly" (Freitag et al. 2005).

"Caballero Montado a l a Brida/Cavalryman Mounted in the La Brida Style Circa 1598"

"War horses gave the Spanish *conquistadores* a decided advantage over the Native American warriors of the New World by providing them with speed, agility, and the leverage of height. These horses belonged to a breed known today as the Spanish Barb, first introduced to Spain by the Phoenicians in ancient times and reintroduced by the Moors after the conquest of A.D. 711.

Barbs are exceptionally intelligent and agile horses standing 55 to 57 inches in height and weighting approximately 800 to 975 pounds. Their short legs, well-muscled chests and sturdy frames made them ideal for cavalrymen. Fewer than 200 Spanish Barbs exist in the United States today.

Because of the expense of war horses the *conquistadores* used leather or steel horse armor to preserve their investment. Coronado was once charged with having stolen a Barb valued at 100 doubloons in gold bullion, an amount worth approximately $6,000 at the current price [1983] of gold" (The Albuquerque Museum. Unpublished exhibition text for the exhibit, Four Centuries: A History of Albuquerque [1983]).

"Caballero Montada a la Brida/ Cavalryman
Mounted in the la Brida Style, circa 1598."
(Courtesy of The Albuquerque Museum of Art and History)

EPILOGUE

On September 18, 1997, a short time after our first Wilbur-Cruce foundation mare, Tubac, had taken up residence at our little ranchito in the Catalina Mountains northwest of Tucson, I decided to call Eva Antonia Wilbur-Cruce. It seemed so easy all of a sudden. Call information, get the number, and call on the telephone. I was nervous. What was I going to say to the author of "A Beautiful Cruel Country" and the person who fought for her little rock horses all her life?

She picked up the phone and I tried to explain that I just got one of her old ranch horses and that I would like to meet her. She misunderstood, my German accent adding to the confusion and she said, "I have no more horses for sale." Finally she put her nephew Al on the phone. I explained to him, he explained to her, and yes, she would love to meet me. How exciting!

Her little ranchito was past the Yaqui Indian reservation west of Tucson. She sat in a wheelchair after a stroke around 1990. When I met her, she was 93 years old. Eva wore a beautiful brightly colored cowboy shirt, her long fingernails were painted bright red, and so were her lips. Her dark skin was framed by white hair put up in a bun and there were those bright, intelligent, lively, lively eyes! Actually she looked lively and alert like her horses do. I think that if she had long ears, they would have moved around like little antennas, not missing a beat. (I wish I had told her that, she would have loved it.)

She grabbed me, gave me a big kiss, and said "how nice to meet you!" The honor was all mine. She told story after story about the horses on the ranch, "hundreds of horses, couldn't give them away, now, you are interested, how nice."

Eva Antonia Wilbur-Cruce
holding a picture of herself, circa 1990.
(Courtesy of the Tucson Citizen)

Her brown eyes were sparkling, she was full of humor and when I mentioned the 1933 article in the Los Angeles Examiner about neighboring ranchers shooting her horses, she laughed and said 'they didn't write that I shot two of their cows for each horse they shot.' Eva did not seem bitter in any way, but full of life and sharp wit as she recalled her cowboy Luiz Lopez breaking the young horses very gently. "Saddle blanket on, saddle blanket off for a week. Saddle on, saddle off for another week. Bridle on, bridle off for yet another week. Then get on and ride. Best horseman there ever was," she said.

We exchanged photos, I showed her pictures of the various Wilbur-Cruce horse groups, and pictures of my 1200-mile ride twenty years ago. 'Cowboy,' she said and grabbed my hands and smiled.

"These horses are very intelligent horses," she said looking at a picture of Tubac, "too intelligent for many men." (To me this includes women. I still say "what a good horseman" for women and men alike. Sorry if this may be politically incorrect.)

"Too intelligent for many men." Can we, the breeders and keepers of the Wilbur-Cruce horses match that intelligence with our breeding program? I ponder this question a lot. Until 1990 the horses were selected by nature for good conformation, good feet, overall health, adaptability, small, sturdy, quick bodies, easy-keepers (little feed goes a long way) and many more attributes.

Their good mind, naturally calm disposition and people friendliness came to help them when the horses were taken off the ranch in 1990. Trapped at the waterhole, loaded into small trailers, put into pens, moved to new locations, trained to ride, all within a short time. None of the horses panicked in such a new situation and killed or hurt neither themselves nor a person. Remarkable.

People will be tempted to change or "improve" the horses. To my mind what needs to improve is our culling and selection

Lorenzo and José Juan.
(Photo by Silke)

criteria. A horse that we can keep sound with corrective trimming or shoeing, for example, can be a wonderful lifelong riding companion. But he or she should not be bred.

Temptation is high to increase size. In over twenty years of working with the conservation of heritage, locally adapted livestock breeds, this trend has always boggled my mind.

Yet we see it with dog breeds, horse breeds, cattle breeds and many others: we like to change them. No doubt, this might happen over time with the Wilbur-Cruce horses. Taking them out of their habitat on the old ranch and breaking up the breeding groups changes them right there. Don't get me wrong, I don't think change is bad. By no means. Surely the horses changed over the 120 years on the Wilbur-Cruce ranch as well, depending on feed, stallions and some selection. But no matter what, the Spanish horse is a Spanish type. If we want to preserve the original Spanish type that came up from Mission Dolores, then we have to try to be as intelligent as the horses.

Juanita, José Juan and Lorenzo with Silke. (Photo © Steve Hillebrand)

This is where it is important to work within established breed registries. Inspections by a qualified team, continued culling of individuals from the breeding stock pool that do not meet the standard (but are in most cases wonderful riding companions!) and working towards a common goal of preserving the original Spanish Barb type. We can be proud that the Wilbur-Cruce population was accepted by the Spanish Barb Breeders Association in 2005 as one of the original strains of the Spanish Barb horse.

José Juan. (Photo by Silke)

My hope is that this book will serve as a marker in time. Seventeen years after the Wilbur-Cruce horses came off the ranch that shaped them to who they are. They still are the small, sturdy, hard-hoofed, intelligent companion with a wonderful disposition. May this book serve as a snapshot in time, and hopefully there will always be some breeders who keep the Wilbur-Cruce line going for what it was and what it is: shaped by nature.

A few months after my first meeting with Eva Antonia Wilbur-Cruce, our second mare Juanita, a loudly colored pinto with one blue eye and one black eye, had taken up residence with us. I called Eva's house to tell her the news. Eva had just passed away. I was saddened by her passing, but happy to know that she knew that her legacy was alive. Dedicated breeders are continuing the line of the legend of the southwest, the Wilbur-Cruce Spanish Barbs.

We thank Eva for keeping them alive and kicking, against all odds. The story of the Wilbur-Cruce horses is a living example how one person can make a difference through her passion and perseverance, but not to forget to "pass the torch." Had it not been for the networking between biologists, breed associations and conservation groups with Eva Antonia Wilbur-Cruce, who helped place the horses with reputable breeders, this strain would have been lost.

"Throughout history, agriculturalists have been stewards of the genetic legacy passed to succeeding generations. What took centuries to develop can be lost in our lifetime. If lost, it cannot be recreated. Only a commitment to stewardship will protect this genetic legacy for future generations" (American Livestock Breeds Conservancy newsletter, July/August 2006).

The little rock horses live on.

Juanita. (Photo by Richard Felger)

Foundation stallion Tumacacori at the Ladder Ranch, New Mexico. (Photo by Silke)

REFERENCES

Allen, Paul. 1990. Mustang herd near last roundup. *Tucson Citizen*, April 28.

Banks, W. Leo. 1995. The Horses of History. *Arizona Highways*. November: 18-22.

Banks, W. Leo. 2002. La Pistolera. *Tucson Weekly* Vol. 19 (22) August 1–7 and (23) August 8–14.

Bennet, Deb. 1988. *Principles of Conformation Analysis, Volume 1.* Fleet Street Publishing Corp., Gaithersburg, Maryland.

Bennett, Deb. 1998. *Conquerors.* Amigo Publications, Solung, California.

Denhardt, Robert Moorman. 1947. *The Horse of the Americas.* University of Oklahoma Press, Norman.

Dobrott, Janie and Jean Walsh. 1997. Wilbur-Cruce Spanish Horse Update. *The American Livestock Breeds Conservancy News*, March/April: 7.

Dutson, Judith. 2005. *Storey's Illustrated Guide to 96 Horse Breeds of North America.* Storey Publishing, North Adams, Maine.

Edwards, Elwyn Hartley. 1994. *The Encyclopedia of the Horse.* Darling Kindersley Publishing, New York.

Freitag, Peg. Silke Schneider, and Marie Martineau. September 2005. Albuquerque Museum of History, Art and Science. *Spanish Barb Breeders' Association Newsletter.*

Gonzaga, Paulo Gavião. 2004. *A History of the Horse, Volume I, The Iberian Horse from Ice Age to Antiquity.* New Era Printing Company, London.

Graham, R.B. Cunninghame. 1949. *The Horses of the Conquest.* University of Oklahoma Press, Norman. (First published 1930, William Heinemann, England).

Los Angeles Examiner. 1933. Scores of horse reported slain. November 10.

Mead, Jim I. 2004. Ice Age Horses of Arizona and Sonora. *Archeology Southwest* 18(3):2. Center for Desert Archeology, Tucson.

Remington, Frederic. 1979. *The Collected Writings of Frederic Remington.* Peggy Samuels and Harold Samuels, editors. Doubleday, Garden City, New Jersey.

Roberts, Honi. 2006. Path of the Palouse. *Trail Rider Magazine,* January/February.

Ryden, Hope. 1970. *America's Last Wild Horses.* E.P. Dutton & Co., New York.

Spanish Barb Breeders Association. 1983. Stud Book 1972–1982, Vol. 1.

Sponenberg, Phillip D. 1990. Letter to American Minor Breeds Conservancy membership. September.

Sponenberg, Phillip D. 2005. Colonial Spanish Horse Update. Personal communication.

Thompson, Mary Anne. 1992. The Colonial Spanish Horse. *Conquistador Magazine,* June/July: 21-22, 24, 26, 42-43.

Turner, Tom. 1990. Spanish horses in dilemma at Arivaca ranch. The *Arizona Daily Star*, 9 9B and 13B.

Wilbur-Cruce, Eva Antonia. 1987. *A Beautiful Cruel Country.* University of Arizona Press, Tucson.

ACKNOWLEDGEMENTS

I thank all the wonderful people who have helped preserve, promote, and love the horses. Special thanks to Eva Antonia Wilbur-Cruce and Paul Allen, Mike Bruce, Sandy Bruce, Robin Lea Collins, Rose Collins, Heidi Collings, Jerold Collings, Jerry Dixon, Marjorie Dixon, Janie Dobrott, Steve Dobrott, Richard Felger, Peg Freitag, Christine Frye, Fred Frye, Gil Gillenwater, Jeanie Griffin, Larry Griffin, Steve Hillebrand, Kay Hughes, T.R. Hughes, Jill Janis, Marie Martineau, Don Miller, Ronnie Monroe, Sisty Monroe, Claire O'Neil, William "Bill" Sanders, Phil Sponenberg, Gunilla Tamm, Marye Ann Thompson, Tom Vezo, Jean Walsh, Michael F. Wilson, Francis Yourstarshining, Kaye Guerin Yourstarshining, Al Zimmerman, and Robert Zimmerman and family.

I thank the Albuquerque Museum and the Arizona Historical Society for archival assistance. Thank you American Livestock Breeds Conservancy, Horse of the Americas, Spanish Barb Breeders Association, Southwest Spanish Mustang Association, and Spanish Mustang Registry for helping the Wilbur-Cruce horses.

WEBSITES OF INTEREST

American Livestock Breeds Conservancy — www.albc-usa.org

Das Berberpferd — www.berber.de

Drylands Institute — www.drylandsinstitute.org

Horse Breeds of the World — www.imh.org/mh/bw/home2.html

Horse of the Americas — www.horseoftheamericas.com

The Long Riders Guild — www.thelongridersguild.com

Rare Breeds International — www.rbi.it

Southwest Spanish Mustang Association — www.southwestspanishmustangassociation.com

Spanish Barb Breeders Association — www.spanishbarb.com

Yourstarshining Studio — www.yourstarshining.com

GLOSSARY

Appaloosa	a breed of light horse developed in the United States by the Nez Percé of Idaho. The Appaloosa is characterized by a spotted pattern of markings. It most commonly has solid-colored foreparts and small, dark, round or oval spots over the loin and hips.
Bay	a tan or red-brown coat color with black points (mane, tail, and lower legs).
Buckskin	the horse has a tan or gold-colored coat with black points (mane, tail, and lower legs).
Cannon	a bone in hoofed mammals that extends from the knee or hock to the fetlock; especially the enlarged metacarpal or metatarsal of the third digit of a horse.
Chestnuts	flattened, oval masses of horn on the medial surface of the forearm and the hock.
Croup	the area from the highest point of the hindquarters to top of the tail.
Dun	a coat color, generally a yellow, always with a brown stripe from the wither to the tail butt.
Ergots	the ergot is thought to be another vestige of a toe similar to the chestnut. It grows from the rear underside of the fetlock joint.
Feathering	the long hair on a horse's legs: fringes of hair on the legs of some horses.
Fetlock	a term used for the metacarpo-and metatarso-phalangeal joint of large animals.
Forelock	the most anterior (front) part of the mane, hanging down between the ears and onto the forehead.

Frog	a V-shaped pad of soft horn between the bars on the sole of the horse's hoof.
Grullo	a slate or mouse-colored horse.
Hands	unit of measurement of height in a horse at the withers; hands high, abbreviated hh. 1 hand = 4 inches.
Hock	the ankle joint.
Overo	refers to a pinto coloration pattern of white over dark body markings in horses. Overos often have fully blue or partially blue eyes.
Paint	a breed of horse with spotted coloring.
Palomino	not a breed of horse but a color type of gold with white mane and tail.
Pastern	the segment of the limb between the fetlock and hoof.
Poll	top of head.
Quarter Horse	an American breed of compact build and muscular hind quarters. Primarily a cattle horse but also used in short sprint races.
Roan	a coat color consisting of a relatively uniform mixture of white and colored hairs; typical colors are red-roan, blue-roan, chestnut-roan.
Tobiano	Tobiano coloring is the inverse of Overo spotting. Tobianos have a vertical spotting pattern, large, rounded spots, more white than dark, white that crosses the back, dark heads, but mostly white legs and white or multi-colored tail.
Withers	the region over the backline where the neck joins the thorax and where the dorsal margins of the scapulae lie just below the skin.

BIOGRAPHY

Silke Schneider was born and raised in northern Germany. She ran away with a traveling circus, trading her homeland for travels and adventures around the globe, including a 1200-mile solo ride on her Arab horse Samir over the old cowboy trails. In 1984 she found her heaven on earth in southern Arizona, where she has lived and worked ever since.

Her passion in life has always been the well-being of animals, which implies they are adapted to their environment. She has been an advocate for preserving old breeds of livestock, also known as heritage breeds, for over 25 years.

She is founder and director of Desert Heritage Breeds under the umbrella of Drylands Institute in Tucson.

From 1992 to 1996 she attended the University of Arizona and earned a degree in Animal Science. Since then she has advanced her degree and now holds an additional degree in education.

She serves on the Board of Directors for the American Livestock Breeds Conservancy, Rare Breeds International, and is vice president of the Spanish Barb Breeders Association.

In 2004 she was elected a fellow of the Royal Geographical Society in London.

Since 1997 she lives with her partner botanist Richard Felger, six Wilbur-Cruce horses, dogs, cat, chickens, turkeys, emus, tortoises and many beautiful plants on their ranchito north of Tucson.